Pillow Thoughts IV
Stitching the Soul

Pillow Thoughts IV

Stitching the Soul

Courtney Peppernell

Andrews McMeel
PUBLISHING®

Acknowledgments

This has been an incredible journey, and none of it would have been possible without the support system I have. To every person who has ever been involved with the Pillow Thoughts series, I want to thank you with my whole heart. To James, from where we started nearly a decade ago—just two people with a dream—to where we are now, it has been a real adventure, and I'm excited to see where our journey continues. To Lindsay, I am so thankful we met and even more for all the work you do for the Pillow Thoughts brand. To Briana, it has been a joy traveling with you to events around the world, and we couldn't do them without you. To Elizabeth, thank you for all your help with editing across the Pillow Thoughts series. All your input was invaluable, and I would not have been able to do any of it without you! To Kirsty, Patty, Fred, Holly, the Read Poetry team, Diane, and every person at Andrews McMeel Publishing, you took a chance on one little book, and together we've turned it into a bestselling series. For this, I will always be so humbled and so grateful for all the work you do.

Mum, Dad, Nick, Brie, and my family, you are the light that always keeps me grounded; and whatever I do in this life, I just want to always make you proud. To my dogs, Hero and Dakota, you have kept my feet warm throughout this series, and there isn't a book I have written where you both weren't close by.

To Rhian, the love of my life: We have grown so much together, and your support of not only the books but my dreams means more to me than you will ever realize. You are the inspiration I keep coming back to; you are my forever home.

Finally, to my readers, my jellyfish—you continue to surprise me with just how much these books mean to you. The Pillow Thoughts series has and always will be incredibly important to me, and I'd like to think that the adventures of You the jellyfish will continue in lots of other ways, but most importantly in your hearts. Thank you for your unwavering support, your stories, and your passion for poetry. It is because of you I have found such love within these pages.

All my love forever,
    Courtney

Twitter: @CourtPeppernell
Instagram: @courtneypeppernell
Email: courtney@pepperbooks.org

Before we begin, I'd like to remind you of a story.
Once upon a time, there was a jellyfish called
You.
You had ventured with heart and mind
You had found strength
You had found wisdom
and You had mended the mind.
Now You must become whole and find
light within the soul.
I hate to spoil the ending.
But You
can heal hearts, minds, and souls.

Table of Thoughts

If your soul is grieving

I used to imagine holding hands as we drove
along the highway, onward to the mountains
and the little cabin we had bought for weekends away.
How you would look over at me at every intersection,
smile that smile of yours and say it was the perfect day.

I used to imagine a beautiful afternoon, sprawled out
on a blanket, watching as you poured more wine. And
I would stare at you and dare to wonder how you could
possibly, after all this time still, be mine.

I used to imagine our future with our children
running along the sand, us arm in arm laughing behind.
We'd look out into the bay, and the ships would be sailing by.

I just never imagined one day you would be the ship
and sail away, leaving me and all our plans on the sand.

There were moments when she was younger, filled with thoughts sometimes too much to process and parts too heavy to carry. It would feel as though the weight of the world was too much to grasp, every dream too far to reach, every breath so hollow she began to feel trapped. Being in her skin didn't feel like enough, as though she were merely a stranger with someone else's name, and high school was a collection of days where she was just desperate to fit in. But she rose from those moments, and she collected her thoughts. She became stronger in her skin, and her breathing became steady. She knew that life was more about her own path and her own healing rather than all the things that felt too heavy.

The day we met, you had been honest about the grief you carried. That there were still haunted memories within your heart, that you were unsure if opening yourself up to love would be an adventure you could bear again. But the other night, I had a dream, and we were sitting together at the edge of the world; we looked like two stars burning against the deepest sea of darkness but filled with light at the same time. I had asked you about the day grief arrived, and you said it came as a surprise, that you hadn't been prepared for the way grief could sink its teeth into the very depths of your soul. I had looked at you, searching your face, wondering how I would ever not get lost in your eyes.

"Don't look at me like that," you had said, and for a moment you had turned away, staring out into the universe, as though its weight were pressed against your chest.

And I had asked, "What way am I looking at you?"

"Like you can see all the cracks in my heart," you said. "Like you can see I am about to break."

"Are you?"

You released a breath, a steady stream of stardust, breaking away into the ocean of the night, and you replied, "Some days I remember the touch of the sun, how it warms me, and the other days the tears that fall from my eyes are the only friends I know."

I had smiled lightly and whispered that I had something for you.

"Please," you had begged. "Just know my heart can't take much more."

"I understand," I replied. "But I am only giving you what I know you need."

Your eyes had landed on mine, searched my face for what felt like the end of the universe and home again. "What is it?" you had murmured.

"Time."

Every moment I close my eyes, I picture this: we are on the couch in my apartment, your head on my chest, the lights from the city glinting through the window. A song is playing on an old cassette, and we are laughing, trying to imprint the lyrics into our minds, so that they will forever become our lyrics and our song. When you left, it felt like those city lights had disappeared for weeks. Every day, I would turn the volume all the way up, in the hopes the music would heal my grieving soul. I wrote you letters, asking where you had gone. I included all the lyrics to our song. But the letters were always returned, and so perhaps the lyrics never really meant anything after all.

Some days, I can go hours without thinking about you. Those days pass by like the rush of traffic on an open highway. I am free on those days, a dandelion dancing in the wind. On those days, the emptiness doesn't feel so unforgivable. But then the ache circles back around and I am thinking of you again. Thinking of all the seconds, minutes, and moments I have since spent without you. And more than the ache, I feel guilt. It wells inside me like a storm, with shattering thunder and lightning splitting open the sky. I feel the guilt of knowing I can live—of knowing that I can continue on—without you. That I can laugh and find joy and love and beauty in the world again. Because it shouldn't be possible to go on without you, to move on and let go. But it is; and on the days I am a dandelion, I relish in this hope.

The flowers had begun to grow again the month you left. They looked so beautiful in the yard, but it felt as though I had swallowed the soil and couldn't breathe inside. Exhausted from the four walls of my bedroom and the pillows soaked in tears, I went to the café, had two coffees, and watched the people as they passed by the window. For a moment, I thought I saw you in the crowd outside, but when I blinked you were gone. And I am so sad about the way things ended and all the things we didn't say.

The air feels warmer as ocean spray and oakmoss hang in the air. An empty bottle sits out on the porch as an afternoon thunderstorm rolls in. I watch the bottle as it filled up with rain. It overflows in the same way the pain overflows in my heart. And I am so sad about all the broken memories and how they're tearing me apart.

The leaves are starting to change color, bright orange and yellow. They have your favorite seasonal drink at the café again. I walk past, and it fills my lungs. I see the name scrawled on the menu board, and I always think of you. And I am so sad, because we will never share a cup of coffee together again, and I've lost all the things I ever knew.

The lake has frozen over, and the snow covers the pavement. The stars fill the deepest parts of the night as I try to find comfort in their light. And I am so sad about the way my soul aches to hold you again. But the seasons have kept moving, knowing everything has changed.

Some people don't have a choice
rather than feeling empty
it is easier to be filled with sadness

It is less lonely to have a mind
filled with scattered thoughts
than no thoughts at all

It is far more promising for
hopes and dreams to become
fragments and shadows in between

There are different types of sadness, and they all bring such a deep feeling of loss. Of not knowing how to heal and how to recover. The long nights filled with wondering *why me* and how to rebuild a bridge that has burned to ashes. But someday the nights will get easier, and you will be able to find the joy in things again. Someday you will look back on all the nights you felt so lost, and they will hold meaning for all the new things you have found.

My best friend asked me, "Why do you love her so much when all she does is break your heart? Why do you push everyone else away, just in the hopes that she might stay?" And I didn't know what to say; how could I when I don't know why I let you destroy me. There are nights when I lie awake, staring at the ceiling, wondering if you are even thinking of me. Wasted nights on you. There are days when I look at my phone three, four, ten times, hoping I have a message from you. Wasted days on you. There are moments when I try to think of all the good memories, the memories that justify why you're so beautiful and why you have my heart. But there are none that don't end in arguing or you walking away. It's been forever, and I can't seem to let you go.

If there are days
you feel as though
your heart is too soft
and sensitivity is all
but a heartbreaking curse,
remember how important
it is that your heart grows
with every song, smile, and touch,
because softness is not a curse
but rather a beautiful gift
from the universe.

We look at a haunted house and we are afraid. Do not enter, stay away, go back the other way. I imagine we think of damaged and grieving people as haunted houses. That if we get too close we may see things we do not wish to see. But haunted houses are more than places with aching memories. They are homes needing light, souls needing compassion, beauty needing understanding. Sometimes haunted houses hold memories that need a hand to hold and a welcome back to the neighborhood.

There have been many parts to the heartbreak. The first part, when I felt you pulling away. The second part, when you told me you didn't love me anymore. The third part, my heart breaking, screaming, crying, agonizing. The fourth part, the empty and dark days, the trying to heal but not knowing how to. The fifth part, the realization that you were never coming home. But the saddest part, the part that haunts me the most, is filled with all the things I didn't say. I should have said that we could have made it if only you loved me as much as I loved you. I should have said that I pictured I'd take you out to dinner, watch our favorite movies, cook you breakfast, and live our lives together, and that you ruined all that. But I didn't say any of it, and I know it will haunt me.

Sometimes sadness is feeling like you are too complex for someone to love you. And so, there are moments I want to take you in my arms and whisper that you are not your past. That your scars are not definitions of who you are or how long you can last. To reach for you when the walls feel they are caving in. To remind you a new day is coming and you can start again.

Others have tried to tell me what grief feels like, how to manage the grief in my heart, how to continue on. But grief is not a singular occasion; it does not happen once and disappear. It happens over and over again, stitched into all the things I do. Every time I find a missing sock that belonged to you. Every old photograph and memory. The texts still piled in my phone from you, with the love heart next to your name. A honeybee flies past my window, and all I see is the day at the lake as you danced and laughed and told me honeybees were your favorite. Every time I walk out my front door, knowing that not long ago was the last time you walked out too.

Days after we ended, I wondered how you would feel when people would ask how I was and you would respond with, "I don't know; we aren't together anymore." Weeks after we ended, I wondered how you would feel when people asked what I was doing, and you would respond with, "I don't know; I haven't spoken to her in weeks." Months after we ended, I wondered how you would feel when people would ask about my job, my family, our life, and you would respond with, "I don't know; I haven't seen her in months." It's been a year, and I no longer wonder how you feel or what you say, because we're strangers now. Strangers with fading memories.

As for loss, I know that I have lost you. I know it when I open the fridge and your favorite chocolate no longer sits on the top shelf. I know it when I open the wardrobe and your clothes no longer hang beside mine. I know it when I find something funny and I can no longer share it with you. I know it when I make plans that no longer include asking you. I know it every time I pick up the spare key, because it was the one you returned to me.

The heartache has been measured
      with all the eyes that fall on mine
how they take pity on my loss
      how I try to tell them that I will survive

The grief has been measured
      in all the hands willing to help
to bring leftovers made with love
      how I try to tell them, I can still stand

The pain has been measured
      in all the late-night calls
Asking how I am, if I need anything
      how I try to say, I just need time

The happiness has been measured
      in the years it took to return
But oh, how it did return
      in all the smaller moments it took to learn
      that I still have a beating pulse

The ache is a song that is forgotten on the radio; a house that locks the doors and lets nobody else inside; a sink piled high with dishes; and a bed unmade, pillows on the floor. The ache is the night sky everywhere, roses wilted, weeds growing in between cracks in the pavement, a heart that buries itself deep in the ground while the world continues on. But the ache will find the joy again. It will become a butterfly spreading wings, a flower bed regrowing, rain arriving and filling the lake once more, your soul replenishing and opening up all the windows and doors.

I see you, and I see how much you deserve to be the love of someone's life. To be the light they never switch off, the arms they choose to run to, the eyes they speak of when they talk of the most beautiful thing in the world. You deserve to be treated like your name was the most delicate name they have ever murmured.

Even in the Grief

You can still pull yourself up
in the morning and make your bed
even if your soul is in pieces

You can still go about your day
even if your bones feel heavy
and there aren't any words to say

You can still open the blinds
and watch the sunlight shining through
even if the darkness is what you prefer

You can still live and find
the beauty in the tiny details of the day

The pain changes you,
it makes you grow in ways
you could never imagine.
But so does love and healing.

Recovery is a battle,
no matter how great or how small.
And even if you have these battles
for the rest of your life,
you are *still here* to fight them,
and for that you won the war.

You are never alone
in the things you feel,
especially the sad things.
Sadness was made
so the soul could learn to heal.

I am sorry that the sadness can be loud and disruptive. I am sorry that it can dictate your days and remind you of old wounds and the pain that always stays. But in the middle of the fight, I hope you notice small flowers growing in the cracks, reminding you that eventually all things return us to the light.

I knew my heart was healing when I stopped going to the places I thought you would be. I stopped getting coffee at your favorite café in the hopes you might be getting coffee too. I stopped driving the long way to work just because it passed by your house and I hoped you'd be out on the front lawn. I stopped going to the Italian restaurant down the street, thinking maybe you would be eating there for dinner. I stopped going to the bar in the city just to see if you were out drinking with friends. I thought maybe if we ran into each other, you would realize the mistake you made and we could be together again. But it wasn't a mistake. You knew what you were doing. And while it took me a little while to catch up, I know it was the right thing too. We belong to different forevers. My heart and your heart were never meant to be together.

The flowers started to reappear in May, and all the snow began to melt away. I wondered where sadness went in the seasons it was not needed. I wondered where pain returned to after one ached for so long. And so I started to realize that grief never truly leaves us. It is often the things we do not wish to feel that are the best things to help us heal.

Grief really just wants to be loved. It hides in the corners of your soul that feel the most vulnerable. It dreams of a moment you will reach out your hands and let it be held. It gathers in the folds of your sheets and asks to be nurtured. Grief knows that ripping yourself apart isn't going to heal the wounds. It is just an ache that needs a place to go. Grief is just a friend needing to be reminded it is not alone.

Somewhere in the world, someone is scribbling thoughts in their journal, wiping the snow off their front windshield, or throwing sticks to their dog on the beach. Somewhere, someone is having their first kiss, their first promotion, their first heartbreak. Maybe someone isn't happy with their life or they want to change something about it. And that's the beauty of it; at any given time, someone is living a life you could live too.

Sometimes the person you thought you needed really isn't. So, you will try to justify all those reasons, and at 2 a.m. you will hope that that person may change. This is what breaks our soul. It breaks us to know that our heart is trying to accept what our mind has known all along. And so we continue, hoping we will wake up one day and that person really will be everything we needed. But life doesn't happen this way. You can love someone more than you have loved anyone or anything in your whole life, but it doesn't mean that person is what you need. Sometimes it's the opposite. Sometimes that person is exactly what you don't need.

You will have your heart broken by someone you trusted, and you will wonder what you did wrong. You will wonder if your broken heart will ever mend itself, if the holes and the cracks will ever seal themselves again. On the more difficult days, it won't even be about the heartbreak itself; it will be about the *way* your heart was broken. It will feel as though you are the only person in the whole world to have felt such sadness, but you must remember that other people exist with broken hearts and carry on. You must learn that if we break our arm, it will never really heal to the way it was before. It will still hurt a little when the weather gets cold, but you continue to learn to stitch things together again. You continue to strengthen once more.

It's not even cutting the thread that's so painful, it's all the memories that spill from the thread. How they tied us together, how they weaved stitches into our very soul. It's not always that the person will no longer be there, it's all the memories that stay—where do they all go?

My heart is a mess; my soul, empty. You walked into my life and made promises you could not keep. The way you drained the hope from my body and left holes in spaces that once felt so alive. Now I'm in a war, trying to stitch together broken pieces and scrubbing the memories from my skin. It's enough to cry under my blankets and wonder why I let you in.

Two coffee cups sat on the table
side by side.
But they were empty,
        drained.
Like our love,
        it was all gone.

I want to close my soul,
        turn off all the thoughts.
Because, lately, I can't breathe.

We said we'd grow old together,
but now
        I'm just frozen in time.

We had all these plans,
but now
        the future isn't so clear.

We said we'd be forever,
        but you left,
and we ran out of time.

I am still trying to understand how we can think so highly of someone else and so little of ourselves. So, when it feels like every breath leaves a bruise and your hopes are set on the love returning, just know that I wish I could hold you when the darkness feels too great. I wish I could comfort you and remind you the sun will reappear. I wish you could see that all the scars are a reminder; you will survive the ache.

If you are looking for respect
tell yourself you are beautiful
every day in the mirror

If you are looking for the truth
remind yourself you are strong
every day out loud

If you are looking to be proud
remember you are not worthless
remember you are not weak
hold yourself piece by piece

If you are looking for hope
I am telling you that the road
always starts again
no matter how long
no matter how far

She will grow from the heartbreak. She will remember how she felt each night you said you'd stop by and never showed. She will smile, radiant when she meets someone new. And she will laugh; it will ring out and be heard for miles. More than that, she will carry herself differently, with confidence, around her this mesmerizing glow. And you'll realize you don't deserve her, because you were stupid enough to let her go.

So, it's been a rough week. Too many storm clouds and people getting under your skin. Too many moments you felt the anger rage, so you have forgotten where to begin. And so you blame yourself for things always going wrong, because what's happening to you couldn't possibly be happening to someone else. It's all your fault when life seems to be spiraling out of control.

Stop and breathe.

You *do* have time to breathe, so make time. Concentrate on the way your body feels when you are breathing in and out. How it rolls over your stomach, catches in your chest, and releases through your lips. A rough week is just a rough week. We all have them; we all blame ourselves when things go wrong. We can't always control the moments that make us feel so alone. But we can control our breathing.

Just stop and breathe.

Some stories *fit* between pages of grief and despair, and others *rise* above the pages. They float under lights, swirling, ascending, transcending. Make a list of all the things you feel. I hope your soul finds relief.

I know how it hurts to be taken for granted. To lose everything you thought you wanted. If I were you, I'd put myself first. Take back all the things I wanted to do. If I were you, I'd take this as an opportunity to rise above it all. But I'm not you, and I can't make choices for you. But I can listen and remind you that the things that make you ache aren't always good for you.

The sunflowers in my garden
rose taller and taller
as the months went on,
always reaching for the sun.
This is how you heal.

By always reaching for the light.

Forever isn't always forever. Sometimes it is two weeks and you thought you had found the love of your life. Sometimes it is a handful of months and you moved in together, full of excitement for the future. Sometimes it is years and you built a home and created dreams together. It still feels the same when it ends. Loss isn't always measured in how many seconds, days, or weeks you knew someone. Forever could have been packed into a dozen memories or spread out over a lifetime of moments; if it ends, the loss feels the same.

I look for you in the quietest hours of the night, hoping that your voice will whisper through the dark that you are still there. I reach for you in the earliest moments of the morning, hoping it had all been but a nightmare. I search for our love all through the day, wondering if you would only give me a sign, then perhaps you would return.

One day, grief wrote me a letter. It said, "All I've ever wanted is the best for you, for you to be patient when I am relentless." It said, "I wanted to teach you to be compassionate, even in the moments when I don't seem fair." It said, "I wanted to remind you that it is impossible to live a life without me." It said, "Sometimes I will be heavy; often I will be small; and other times, I will make you feel so empty, it will feel impossible not to fall." And then it said, "I want you to know it is not because I don't love you or that I don't want you to win. It's because I need you to know that without me, you wouldn't let anything else in."

If your soul is lonely

I've been missing you all this time, and I can't see an end to all this loneliness. It hurts to watch as you love someone else while I still think about all the moments that used to be mine. I can't keep the ache silent, not while I'm thinking about you after coffee or right before I sleep. We threw caution to the wind, went there when all our friends said not to. Maybe this is karma for not just turning the other way. But I was so lonely, and your smile made me forget all the words I wanted to say.

Loneliness isn't always wanting to find romantic love. It can be wanting to find a friend. When all you want is someone to call, someone to get dinner with on a Friday night because you're bored. Someone to laugh with, rely on, be on the same page with. Sometimes I don't want a therapist to talk to; I just want a friend.

You broke me, and now I can't feel a damn thing. I'm trying to convince myself the light is under all the scars. But I'm torn up, and it all hurts too much. The truth is, I never knew dancing with you would lead to this. I'm chasing someone who isn't here anymore, a shadow of a love that walked out the door. I am so lonely, I don't think I can take this anymore.

We've been sleeping
next to each other,
but we're miles apart.
I know I need to say
goodbye,
but walking even a mile
on my own scares me.

The parts you struggle with
are the parts of you
that need the most love

The parts that feel so lost
are the parts of you
that need the most kindness

The parts that trouble you
are the parts of you
that make you the most brave

The moon continues to shine light even when she is quarter, half, or full. Even when the stars hide behind the clouds and she is shining lonely in the dark. She still shines. So, when you are near empty, remember your worth, because the universe always needs your light.

Listen to your soul,
how it calls your name
in the darkest hours of your life.
Your soul knows you better than anyone;
nurture it, find things that help it grow.
Find moments that make it whole.

One day, you will be someone who believes in yourself. You will conquer the thoughts of doubt and win the battle you face with your mirror. You will realize strength is not in the breaking or the falling but in the quieter moments when you look at how far you've come and how much you are healing.

The body will feel like a landslide in the middle of all the loneliness. You'll feel the earth slipping away from you as you try to hold yourself together. But sometimes it's better to let all the darkness slip away; and underneath the rubble, a new you will rise, full of hope and knowing all pastures are restorable.

The stars have seen so much of me: my first kiss, my first broken heart, my tears as I looked out into the quiet, still lake. How I need them more than ever, to shine light over me. But I know that eventually we have to face the things that make us afraid, even if those things are the aching, lonely pieces of ourselves.

The hurt leaves eventually. It may return from time to time to remind you of the lessons you learned. But one day, your chest won't feel so heavy. You won't feel exhausted just at the thought of putting on your shoes and starting another day.

Language is sometimes being able to speak what motivates someone else. It's determining what they are passionate about, what gives them hope, what doesn't make them feel so alone, what they live for.

Losing is never easy. You lose a game, a lover, a piece of you. It takes grace and humility to claw your way back. But when you experience loss, you experience the determination for better days. And determination is a very powerful thing.

You should start with the way you want to feel. If you want to feel alive, feel capable, feel courage. Once you start with yourself, you can handle the rest.

They call it the lonely hours, when everyone is asleep but you're awake, wondering if they'll stop by before the sun rises. But if they were worth it, they'd already be next to you, and it wouldn't be called the lonely hours.

"I wish you the best"
   were the last words I ever said to her
and it's taken me all this time
   to mean them

It's about learning to find the comfort in all the quiet. To finding bravery in being by yourself, to mending the ache with kindness to your heart and forgiving yourself on the days you fall apart. It's about knowing, for all the lonely days with this struggle, there are days full of hope coming.

I poured myself into you
every dream and every hope
And yet you walked away
the minute I needed help

You can't always see someone who is struggling. Sometimes it's obvious, like when his eyes are red, and the bottle of whiskey is half empty. Or maybe she's on the train and she bursts into tears. But other times it's quiet, like when he won't smile or speak for weeks, locking himself in his room; or she hides behind books in the library, trying to find the one that promises, again she will bloom. Whether loud or quiet, strange or familiar, be kind to other people's struggles. Underneath all the mess, they are waiting for hope. They are waiting for a happy ending to their stories. Be hope to somebody.

I hope the younger you would be proud of the struggles you've survived and the twists and turns you've overcome. I hope the younger you knows the battles you've won and the lessons you've learned. You've made it this far; be proud of who you are.

You are going to meet someone, and you'll count all the moments until you get to see them again. More than that, they'll remind you why your heart had to break and bend before you found a love too pure to comprehend.

It is your right to create safe spaces for yourself. No matter how much you want to fix or save someone, you cannot compete with toxicity. People who are no good for us have ways of pretending they are. But life is not meant for pretending; it's too short for such long moments of struggling. As hard as it may be to let go, you have to move to safer grounds.

Time doesn't always completely heal us, but it does make the ache easier to live with. But so does making your bed and opening the curtains every morning. So does not shouldering so much weight of the troubles of others. So does a smoothie in the summer and a mug of cocoa in winter by the fire. So does painting, drawing, writing, documenting your life. So does listening to yourself, following your instincts, and controlling your impulses. Broken hearts from friends or lovers will frequent in your life, but surround yourself with the simple things that make your heart beat.

Ever After

You don't have to settle for familiarity or continue with
old habits. You don't have to be the second choice, or the
leftovers, or the one who is always just there. You deserve to
be what someone has always dreamt of, someone who lights
up every room, someone who is cared for, cherished, held the
way the sky holds the moon. You deserve someone who will
look at you and say, "I'm so lucky."

You deserve to be an ever after.

But I'm human
and you're human
and sometimes
we get drunk
on our own loneliness
and forget
we have the power to heal.

She just wants someone to spend Friday nights with, someone who will let her dance the night away and come home with her. She just wants someone to fill all the lonely space, who reminds her life isn't a race but a home to build and a purpose to fulfill. She just wants someone who will make the effort, love all her flaws, support her through it all.

It's not that I have closed myself off or that I've changed. I've just been hurt too many times before. Giving to people who waste my compassion becomes exhausting. My happiness is important. The happiness of the ones I love is important, and I've lived enough time on this earth to not allow anybody to try and ruin that.

Growing from struggles, lost friendships, and self-destruction doesn't mean changing who you are. It means learning yourself over, figuring out what makes you the best you that you can be.

I have miles to go
   before I lay my head
   to rest

I have seasons to live
   before I regrow
   and blossom

I have caution to throw
   to the wind
   before I keep my promises

The voice may never go away; it will creep into your bedroom in the middle of the night, whisper that you are worthless and can't do anything right. But you are louder than the voice, you are stronger than the things keeping you down. You exist because you deserve to be here.

The setbacks will come. Whether you are mentally prepared or not, they will come. Because this is life. You will be disappointed in the things you do—maybe studying is too difficult, maybe you didn't get that job, maybe you broke someone's heart or they broke yours, maybe you feel lonelier than you have ever felt. But the thing to remember most is you are always in your own corner. Cheer yourself on in the times it feels too hard to carry on. Hold yourself to a standard to keep going; you are more than the challenges you face, more than the struggle of life. You are a golden opportunity to make things right.

Sometimes two people fall out of love. There isn't anyone to blame, it's just things don't stay the same. It doesn't make sense, and you'll spend your moments with a mile of what-ifs. But even while the best intentions aren't always enough, it doesn't mean you aren't. Healing starts when you stop blaming yourself or the love that went wrong. You can mend, all on your own.

Loneliness often hurts. It suddenly becomes hard to put on shoes and carry on with your day. It feels as though your heart has split in two, and your jagged edges make the world seem frightening. But this is when you need the light of the day most. Love the earth in the way it loves you. It will get easier with every breath.

If I could lay all my memories out on a table in photographs, there would be some I wish I could take away. But the most important thing I've learned is that in each one I'm never alone. In every photograph, I've come to always find my way home.

In the quiet hours, when darkness creeps in and the loneliness surfaces and chooses to begin, I want you to know that, while I hope many things for you, more than anything, I hope that feeling part of something special within these pages—a journey, a promise, a place to begin—always reminds you of a home we have built out of thinking of each other.

If your soul is searching

Every item abandoned in the lane comes with its own story, a hidden message to the pain. Broken bottles and worn-out furniture, forgotten toys and empty bags. There is very little difference between your riches and their rags.

We kissed, and you laughed because you had never kissed a friend before. I was nervous because all I've ever wanted is to be something more. And I should have told you how soft your lips were, but I didn't, because part of me knew you were thinking about her.

I always knew when you were at home because there would be fresh coffee brewed and the bed made. All our pictures on the walls of a life we used to live, of all the beginnings and firsts we shared. But now there is no coffee in the pot, and the bed isn't made, and all the photos on the walls are just memories that will eventually fade.

She's been packing suitcases all her life, running from country to country to soak in all the new sites. She's been meeting new people but refusing to get close. And in all the adventures and all the excitement, all she's ever wanted was for someone to give her a reason to stay.

You can't carry people on your shoulders
when you are searching for your own soul
This journey is about you
How you carry your own legs
and climb your own mountains
This is about finding your voice
and letting it shine through loud and clear

We were blowing bubbles in the middle of the field. Laughing about things that reminded us of our childhood and everything we used to be. Once upon a time, you had my heart, and I had yours, but not all things work out the way we want them to. But I'm glad we still managed to stay friends. I'm glad after all the hurt, when I asked if you would leave, you said, "I wouldn't dare."

Sometimes closure doesn't happen right away, but rather later on. And you might not notice for a while until a friend points out that you're smiling again. That you are laughing and not breaking every time you hear their name. It's about coming home after a very long and exhausting adventure. It's about finding your soul when you thought it had gone forever.

I am searching for something soothing and comforting. Something that doesn't make my heart feel like a rock, heavy in my chest. Something that gives me back my resilience.

The wild air and the smell of lavender is enough to bring me back to life. When nature calls, I follow, no matter how blind my heart feels.

We hold ourselves back sometimes, probably because we are afraid of the outcome. But life is about taking risks, jumping, even if you may fall. If you stay stagnant your whole life, you'll never grow into your full potential.

You were someone before your soul went missing. You are still someone while you are out searching. You are more than a forgotten road to an empty house. You are the entire highway, the whole map, the footprints leading you home.

She wanders through towns as much as she wanders through hearts. Never one to stay in a place for too long. And when asked how she will possibly build a home, she says, "I have the sky, the mountains, and the trees. I am never on my own."

There is no time limit on realizing what you have lost. Some realize right away, and for others it takes longer. But they will realize when all the dust settles and the anger subsides; they will realize they have lost you. And the emptiness will hurt them more than they ever hurt you.

We started at sunrise, on a stretch of highway leading us to the mountains. And I could hear my name being called through the wind, the clouds whispering the secrets of the forests. The sun willing to be our guide. Adventure awaited, and I was tired of all the fear. There would be no more hiding.

She is not confined by time
she is a running river
seeking freedom to flow through life
unchained

Heartbreak was once sending a letter and never receiving one back. Now it's texting and having the message read and never replied to. It's still the same feeling. Rejection hurts. Being ignored hurts.

How delicate your skin
to cover a soul full of fears and complexities
it doesn't matter to me about your color
but rather all your hopes and how true we stay to each other

If anything
be curious about
the next day
What it may
          bring
The doors that may
          open

There will be moments you wish you had an endless amount of. Moments you wish never had to end, adventures you wish could go on forever. And these are the moments you live for. A pink sky that lasts an extra few minutes; a field of flowers in full bloom; a clear, dark night to count the stars. Enjoy these moments, savor them, store them in your mind forever.

You find inspiration in adventure. But adventure doesn't have to always be climbing mountains and trail blazing through ancient pathways. Sometimes adventure can be sitting in an armchair, watching the fire turn to embers, and realizing no matter where you are, you will rise from the ashes.

Undress me
not my clothes
but rather

      my fears
      my walls
      my doubts

Undress me
and turn me
inside out

The garden needs
    unearthing
time for fresh soil
dig out all the weeds
plant more flowers
watch all the new colors
start to regrow

Sometimes an awfully big adventure
is to stay inside
look at yourself in the mirror
and ask
has my soul grown

Life is meant to be lived one adventure to the next. Despite how small some adventures can be, they all mean something. Trips to the supermarket when it's cold out, holding hands in line for a movie, studying by yourself in the corner of the library. All the small moments are strung together like fairy lights in the courtyard of a bar. When you have lived your life, it will be these small moments that matter.

There we were, across from each other, and I'd never seen anyone more magical than her. She had her laptop, and I my notebook. Both lost in what we were doing. But I think that's love, when you can be lost together.

You finally start to learn who you are when you are a teenager, and suddenly the years go by in the blink of an eye and you are graduating as an adult, even if you are still looking at all the parts of yourself and asking why. But no one ever told you how badly someone can break your heart or that sometimes our friends don't always stay our friends. No one ever told you that you can be happy and sad at the same time or just because someone is smiling doesn't mean they're fine. The people around you spoke of responsibility and growing up, but it never meant anything until now. Now it's real and it's scary, and it doesn't feel like an adventure you want to begin. But you will learn, and you will find your way. Despite all the obstacles and how difficult it can be to live in a world where you are the maker of your own destiny, just remember that transformation starts with surrendering and ends in bravery.

I want to know about your dreams and listen to you talk about your day. I want to hear your childhood stories and what makes your heart race. I want you to tell me your fears and trust me with your secrets. I want to listen to your favorite music while we lie in the middle of your bedroom floor and kiss until we can't think anymore.

It started at a bar: I saw her across the room, and I knew if I wanted to dance with anyone it was the girl who reminded me of the moon. Late at night, driving in her old car, making out to songs on the radio, I think I'm falling in love, but I don't know. My heart was in my chest over a girl I'd just found, but it was 3 a.m. and I was telling her all the things I'd never said out loud. She put her arms around me and made me feel less alone; and in that moment, I was reminded that a person can be both an adventure and a home.

And when the universe gave us life and told us to walk the earth, I am sure she wanted us to spend more time searching for the joy in the things that light up our soul. Rather than seeking validation in what others think or assume without knowing our whole story. Because others who don't know you don't know the stories inside you or the hopes and dreams your soul dares to have. Others cannot see the beauty and the strength that overflows inside your heart. Spend more time walking this earth with your head held high, your dreams flowing from your veins, and less time letting precious moments pass you by.

Soul-searching is not a race
We never begin in the same place
Or run at the same speed
We rarely end up at the same finish line

You run your own race
And match your own speed
You finish at your own line

There comes a point when you stop operating at the same frequency. When everything you thought you knew becomes just another station to tune in to. Soon, you realize there is more, that there *always* will be more. That you will continue growing and evolving and changing. As a result, your habits change, you walk in and out of people's lives, and they walk in and out of yours. You find wonder in different things. You grow to love things you never thought you would. Our souls are not meant to operate at the same frequency all our lives; they are meant to create waves.

The most beautiful thing is listening to stories come from the soul. The way someone's face lights up when they speak of the things that drive them and complete them. Or of the dreams they have, the hopes they wish for, the changes they want to make to the world. I get dizzy off other people's passion. I see stars in the eyes of people who want to make a difference. I have a place in my heart for the people who choose kindness every time they start a new day.

The search
will take
your light,
your patience,
your breath

But the awakening
will restore
your grace,
your endurance,
your hope

Not all people find themselves while on the road. Some have been to the center of bustling cities and the deepest hidden places in quiet towns, and they are still searching. It won't matter how many stamps are in your passport. The journey starts and ends with you. I will give you moments that take your breath away. I will go with you through times you did not think you would ever see. I will remind you to laugh and to hold on to memories. I will pray the world moves to give everyone the basic rights and needs to be free. I will work to make you believe in the beauty of the earth; and in the end, when you return home, I will hope you have found your worth.

If your soul is whole

More than anything, I am in love with the way you carry your heart. How you hope for better things and dream of a life that is a little less confusing. My love for you exists in all the veins of my heart—twisting, wielding a path to my soul.

We were headed to the lake—just a weekend vacation away. Your feet were on the dashboard of my car, your hair moving in the wind, our favorite song playing on the radio. And I remembered meeting you all those months ago, how my chest felt tight almost all the time, and my body ached of all my life's memories I'd left behind. And now, how you are my breath of fresh air, my shoulder when I need to cry, my ear when I need someone to listen. No more aching or doubting, just the view of you, my heart pounding. If this is what love is, then mine for you is greater than this universe.

There are people who have always loved the forest, no matter if the trees are full or bare. That's the kind of love you deserve. Someone who loves you in every season.

For years, I have been a building, with empty spaces and corners where the light barely touches. I have been full of dust and darkness, my heart uninhabitable. But then I met you, and you made the days feel warm and planted gardens in my bones, and suddenly you turned me back into a home.

The human heart is controlled by an electrical system. It is the reason your heart has rhythm. Funny, isn't it, how when I met you I could feel the electricity beating through my heart. As though suddenly I had given all control to you.

I want to know everything, but maybe not all at once. When you broke your arm rolling down a hill. How you were stung by a bee in third grade and cried. The doubt you feel before you take on your greatest challenge. If you've felt alone. What it means to you to create a home. I want to know the things that make you feel like you are enough; I want to be that love. I want to know all the things that make up who you are, and I want to learn about them for the rest of our lives.

I am not sure how everything about us makes so much sense, but it does. When the light catches your eyes, I know what it means to love the sun. When I reach for you in the dark, knowing I am reaching for someone beautiful, I know what it means to love the shadows. When every color starts to bleed into one, I know what it means to love the universe. I can't pretend to understand everything in this life, but I understand my love for you.

My wish for you is to feel me near you wherever you go. That you feel me in the stars as you look at the night sky, that you feel me in the breeze as you drive in the open among these old oak trees. That in your dreams you won't think of our love as bittersweet, or painful, or too hard to go on. Instead you will feel our love, running, rushing like water along the river. And all the roses I've ever given you will bloom rather than wither.

The stars and colors you see
when you rub your eyes
are called phosphenes.
I wonder what it is called
every time I close my eyes
and I see your face in the stars
and our love in the colors.

You deserve someone who loves you in every heartbeat.
Someone who thinks about you at one point or another
during their day and doesn't punish you on the days you aren't
feeling okay. You deserve someone who listens as you talk
about your interests, who will motivate you to always strive.
You deserve someone who makes you feel alive.

There are moments our love feels like the world—
unpredictable, unforgiving, unstable. But I am reminded
that in the world there is also light and trees that grow again.
So, my love for you continues to grow, continues to move
through every turn and every bend.

You have left your
    fingerprints
across my body
and all over my heart.
Even in the moments
    we are apart,
I still feel your touch.

We spent that rainy afternoon making origami at your coffee table. You made dragons and love hearts, swans and roses. And then you made a paper crane, told me to make a wish; but you had forgotten I'd made my wish long before. And oh, how it came true, how I'd always longed for someone like you.

You said nothing. But it wasn't the bad kind of nothing. It was the kind of silence that caused fireworks. Invisible tethers sprouting from our hearts and joining us together.

Find the person who makes your body fold and collapse against their touch. Find the person who wants to grow with you, learn with you, keep you safe. Find the person who makes you see stars every time you kiss. Find the type of love that makes you want to exist.

We were sitting in your car, watching the waves roll toward the beach, and the sun was sinking, colors splayed across the sky. And you asked me if I had ever heard of a double sunset. You said the theory was really just a planet orbiting two stars. But when you looked at me, the fading light of this world catching in your hair, you said you'd rather believe a double sunset was just two suns going to sleep in each other's arms.

Love someone the way you love the little things in life. A few extra minutes in bed, how bread tastes when dipped in soup, fresh air when you've been at work all day. When you love someone like the little moments that consume your day, that love becomes as simple and pure as the sun rising and setting in that magical kind of way.

We will always think of things that break us. But remember to think of the things that make you whole. When you find a passage in a book that speaks to you, a funny comic online, a sunny day in a big city, or the smell of fresh air in a small town. The butterflies you feel for someone who turns your world upside down. Think of the things that make your heart burst with love.

But your heart does more than circulate the life around your body. It feels deeply for words that fit the moment; it treads carefully and carefree, sometimes unsure of what will be. It soaks in reminders, opportunities, things that make it beat. It glows when you are in love and pushes you to stand on your own two feet. It is a friend to your soul when you feel so lost.

The way love has made me fall and break; the way it has made me push boundaries, drive miles; the way love has made me blind. Yet here I still am, breathing, living, loving.

When You Fall in Love

It's falling in love with insecurities
and flaws
knowing you have them too

It's falling in love with their past
because they are now your
present and future

It's falling in love with their hopes
and dreams
and sharing your own too

It's falling in love with every good morning
and goodnight text
because you can't start or end your day
without them

It's falling in love with knowing how much
you care for someone
even if you never thought it was possible

It's a summer's day
and your smile makes
the blood in my veins
run wild

It's a fall day
and your laugh
might be the best sound
in the world

It's a winter's day
and my heart
is not contained
in my rib cage
because of you

It's a spring day
and the way you look
in the early hours of the morning
makes my skin burn in all
the right ways

I think you are
beautiful in all the seasons
But I have been
thinking about you all day
and I just wanted to remind you
how much you take my
breath away

There is something so gentle about the way you take my hand and press your lips to my knuckles. Something so simple, but a love that's given me hope.

There will always be best and worst parts of people. There will always be moments life feels stagnant, unfulfilling, boring. Love is what fills the space between mundane and exciting; it takes hold with such force, it cancels everything out. My love for you is all things: cooking dinner so you don't have to, doing laundry while you are at work, waiting patiently outside the bar for you to pick me up—even if it's three in the morning, you still tell me to call. My love for you is laughing as you kiss my neck, begging me to dance to our song. It's drinking the last of the wine while you wash the dishes at night. For every standstill moment of my life, for every exciting moment, I will love you even more. You are my light, my love, the person always standing on the other side of an open door.

Your ex's name tastes like burnt coffee. And it's not because of you. It's my fault. I feel anger thinking about all the people who haven't treated you in the way you deserve. Who haven't looked at you and seen all the wonder and grace of the universe. I wish I had met you at the beginning of time, told you everything would be all right when your hand eventually found mine.

These moments with my head on your chest, listening to your breathing, your stomach making funny sounds, the TV noise in the background. I live for these moments. I feel your love as you run your fingers through my hair, as you run your nails across my back, drawing on my skin. These simple moments in bed after a long day, when you are holding me, and I just know in the end everything will always be okay.

Make a throne of your heart
    And only allow a queen to take residence

But even if they like different movies, or songs, or books, they should still want to know yours. When someone loves you, they want to know what your favorite things are.

Here you are
despite all your scars
And for all the things I wish for you
I wish more than the sky and its stars
that you love yourself as much as I do

Here you are
like all the colors
melting in the sky
I will always say goodnight
But never goodbye

Here you are
and we've been getting older
Sorting through moments
difficult to define
But you bring the light
and I know it's a sign

Here you are
thinking no one sees your demons
as you fight to keep them at bay
But I see it all
and I promise
I'll return each day

Sometimes I think about
how snow only falls in certain places
or how our thoughts get stored away
in secret spaces.
I think about driving down a highway
with my hand in yours,
with that sleepy smile I adore
and knowing you'll always stay.
I think about the color of your eyes
in summer and your favorite shirt;
it's the one you took from me.
Sometimes I think about things
and everything we can do.
But if I'm honest, the thing
I think about most
is you.

I know we're all just afraid to let someone in. It's when they get too close and knit themselves into our skin. We think, *Where else can we go if we see them in everything?*

I see a universe in you
the way it reflects in your eyes
and in the way you talk
and hold yourself
even in the moments you hide

Out of all these souls
yours makes me fold
and I just want you to know
that you are safe with me
Your heart is a home
I just always want to hold

From here until you will have me
if why I think you are enough
needs reason after reason
I will be here
with my hand over your heart
reminding you season to season

You deserve all the love
a person can possibly have
And every single part of me hopes
you know you are a person
I think the absolute world of

Love is sweats and messy hair. It's cooking together when you're tired after work, and it's walking hand in hand at those little county fairs. It's makeup on pillows and talking late at night. It's falling asleep midconversation and laughing about it the next day. It's showing that you care with texts like "love you" and "be home soon." It's spending weekends sleeping in and watching movies until noon. It's breathing in their scent, and nothing smells as good. It's having someone who always reminds you to just be yourself. It's leaving butter and toast on the kitchen counter for breakfast and making extra dinner so they have leftovers. It's standing in the middle of a crowded room and watching their face light up when they see you. Love is soft lips and wiping away tears. Love is hidden notes and encouragement through the years. Love is wanting their happiness shared with yours. Love is checking in, two souls wrapped together, skin to skin. Love is power, oxygen, everything that is right. Love reminds us of magic, like the stars at night.

If your soul needs empowering

Sometimes I look at you, and I wonder who made you feel like you weren't strong enough to face each and every day. I wonder who made you feel as though you weren't smart enough to go your own way. I wonder what I can do to show you that you do not need to seek shelter in other people's acceptance. You do not need other people's permission to begin. There is a perfectly good home within your own skin.

It takes strength to show kindness to your soul while you are healing. Some of us fear being vulnerable around others. We are so afraid to unmask ourselves and show our true colors to the rest of the world. But there is no shame in recovery. We are only human. We are allowed to make mistakes and learn from them. There is such beauty in redemption. Such wisdom in growing. Be a friend to your heart while it undertakes its journey.

It's not always about telling yourself that you are fearless and radiant and brave. It's about acknowledging all your faults and not despising yourself for them.

People fear those who stand up for themselves. The people who fight day in and day out for the rights of the vulnerable. They fear the people who fight the chains. So, continue breaking them.

You will meet someone, and they will become the person who consumes most of your thoughts. You will envision a future and be consumed by expectations of how it's all going to turn out. You will fall so in love, much of everything else won't matter as such. Until, one day, things aren't going like you planned, and you start to think about your own dreams, but they are nowhere to be found. You start to wonder who you are in the world without this person, but you can't find the answer. To love someone doesn't mean you have to lose yourself. There is great magnificence in knowing your way and not being afraid to leave people behind.

Each new day brings the sun back to us, and we can leave our troubles on the windowsill as the night takes them with her. So, I wanted to remind you that if you feel you can't go on, know that you are needed: who you are, will be, and were.

We don't all live without regret. I always try to see each mistake as a lesson. Something that needed to be taught. But there is one person I deeply regret. And it's not because of how she acted or the lies she told. It's not because of how selfish she was or all the things she thought she controlled. It's because in the process of loving her, I forgot what it was to be me. In the time she acted poorly, I ignored all the signs. And I think that's life's greatest tragedy, when you allow another to treat you badly and your response is "it's fine."

It's about transformation. Instead of finding boredom, find passion. Instead of being discouraged, find encouragement. Sometimes it's not even what you draw from others, it's what you draw from within. Inspiring yourself is a place to begin.

The sun will always carry hope every day it rises. You must learn that it also carries respect, strength, and goodwill. All the things you should take with you as you go about your day. When someone says you are beautiful, capable, strong, and a person who will achieve their dreams, I hope that person is yourself.

In the beginning, there will be more bad days than good. On those bad days, you won't want to get better. You will tell yourself it is easier to stay in pieces. Recovery is not warm tea and a handful of sleepless nights. It is an ache that makes it unbearable to wake up. But it is also finding a new person among the grief of all the pieces. It is never giving up on the road to surviving.

Success is merely how you perceive it to be. You can be in love and be successful, have a family and home that is your own and be successful. You can have a song on the radio, a book in stores, or know all the notes to your mother's favorite song on piano. You can be sober, staying clean and be successful. The world may have defined success, but your gift is to decide what success means to you.

Magic is more than stars,
    her eyes, and dreams

It is standing in the shower
    after a long day,
    exhausted,
    tired from the world,
    in despair

And yet the water feels
    cleansing,
    warm,
    filled with repair

The bravery isn't to stay
    broken
The bravery is to survive

And show off the scars

"Calm down" isn't always what someone wants to hear. Try to remember that, for some people, the illness holds on with all its might. It wraps its jaws so tightly around the heart, it feels impossible to even move. But even if calm thoughts seem unimaginable, it does not mean you cannot live. It does not mean you are useless, replaceable, or unimportant. Because you are stronger than the jaws locked around your heart. You can do anything, my friend.

You can't blame yourself for every mistake you've made. Sure, there will be some you are ashamed of. Maybe you broke that girl's heart, when she was always kind to you. But if you live the rest of your life building a house out of all the mistakes you're ever made, then you are never going to call it a home. Keep your mistakes as lanterns, hanging on the tree outside, a reminder that even error can bring us back to light.

Progress is personal. Someone's biggest accomplishment may be something that came naturally to you. This doesn't make it any less important. People struggle with different emotions and skill sets. How far they have come or how far they have to go is part of their journey. Never diminish someone else's progress.

We lose things all the time: books, sweaters, friends, and love. But losing yourself is a loss of a different kind. If you are out there in the world, searching for who you are, take your time.

Throughout life, lots of people will tell you that they love you. Some will leave no sooner had they told you, others will stay awhile, and a rare few will stay for all your life. But to give love to yourself, that takes diligence, bravery, forgiveness. Anyone can tell the world they love themselves; few actually mean it.

But you notice worth when it is wrapped around someone. It has a different glow. So, I hope you never settle when it comes to your worth. That you know it and acknowledge it and let others see it too. Because who you are and how you shine should be known. You should be taught to understand you are worth the world.

You can rely on yourself, but that doesn't mean you have to reject people willing to help you. There are souls in this life who want what is best for you. Surround yourself with good people. Surround yourself with people who care about what you do.

You don't have to punish yourself for breaking your own promises. But you must try to keep them. If you are trying, you are always keeping that promise.

Life felt simpler when we were younger. We wanted to climb trees and run through sprinklers. We liked to swashbuckle friends and ride bikes in the late afternoon. We liked to be pilots of jungle gyms and pirates of the sea. We liked to be first ladies and magicians and talk to fairies. What inspires children changes when we grow. But maybe as children we really did have all the answers—to be kind to others, to fill our lives with wonder, to fight for the things we believe in, with voices as loud as thunder.

Caring for Yourself

Just remember you are a home
to a soul that needs rest
and sleep and soft words

You are someone else's
memory, friend, family

You are a stranger's glance
a cashier's conversation
a waiter's last patron

You are an atom that exists
in a world constantly on the move
you deserve to value yourself
the way the sky values the moon

You can hold your head up or down, or however the hell you like.
It's your walk.

I remember the fear, how it gripped me when I realized it was much less looking up to women and more about falling for them. The way a woman moves, speaks, thinks. How I wanted my lips on hers, how I wanted conversations late at night and dates over candlelight. The constant feeling of people watching if I went to hold her hand, the wanting to tell the world loving women didn't define me, didn't change who I was, my dreams, my hopes, my drive for life. But then things did start to change. I no more feared what people would say or think because it wasn't going to change the love I felt. I started to believe in the world again, the rise and fall of my chest as I breathed change in. How beautiful it is to change, to be open to things different than what we have always perceived. I started to tell the world I was in love. Because love is a wonderful thing, and love always wins.

She will continue to grow, without all the comments you made about her wearing that dress or how she did her hair. She will find light under all the self-destruction, and she will regain her energy from everything you drained from her. She will find her way back from the despair you stitched into her skin, and you will see a new her begin again without you.

You lose her by never acknowledging she is her own person—a separate existence to you. You bring heartache when you rather control than share. You lose her by never being fair, by taking her for granted instead of showing her she is the best thing to happen to you.

Time and time again,
I am in awe
of a woman's resilience.
How she can take back her
heart and home,
even when it is burned down
again and again.

You are worthy of your story
   It's yours
You deserve to have a stage
   If only one soul to listen

There was a time she measured herself in small steps, rising in the morning to take a shower, filling the empty cupboards with food, remembering to turn the lights back on after weeks of darkness. And now she rises in the morning with purpose, ties her shoelaces the way she tied all the old memories together and forgave them. She looks in the mirror and knows each new day is still a journey, but one worth taking.

When you are whole by yourself, this frightens some people. When you are strong, in spite of suffering, some people don't understand. But carry yourself, anyway, tell your story the way you need to. Every journey is worth knowing, the good, the between, and the harrowing.

You are surrounded by people who are trying to mold you to fit an idea that they perceive as beautiful. You will be expected to smile instead of standing up and fighting harder than most to be a leader. But you were born strong. Never let the world take away your voice.

Courage is not always meant for battlefields. Sometimes courage is found when you see someone else in trouble, and you speak up.

You have to start by not wishing to be somebody else. When you wish to be someone other than yourself, you start to lose who you are. Trying to become someone else is not the same as becoming the best version of yourself.

She had a dream, and in her hands, she was holding her heart. But she remained still, so it crumbled to dust. You need to move. Your heart is broken, not dead. Get up. Open the curtains. You are more than dust. You are a warrior who bled, and your blood is worth every color in the sky.

If I could talk to my younger self, I would tell her to forgive herself. Being soft in a hardened world isn't a bad thing. I would apologize to her for never allowing her to use her voice for fear of what others may say. I would tell her to be braver, live every moment like it's her last day.

I know what it's like to want things all at once. To have your goals achieved in minutes, to be free of all the moments pushing you to your limits. But the journey is part of the lesson. You need to walk the path to find what is in your heart.

Let every moment that pains you
make you stronger and kinder.
The trauma is yours,
but you are not the trauma.

On a rainy Sunday, she took out the pieces of an old jigsaw puzzle and began to piece together a picture of the moon. How it reminded her of her journey, placing each piece of herself back together again. How she hoped to become whole meant becoming her own friend.

You belong to a life filled with experiences that will shape you and allow you to grow your soul. You belong to a life that will show you love, kindness, and courage. Even if there are moments when you feel all things rushing against the current. You belong to a life feeling safe and at peace. You deserve to feel empowered; you deserve to feel like a masterpiece. And more than anything, you deserve to always be yourself.

If your soul needs to breathe

Your true self knows its limitations and its boundaries. Your true self never punishes your soul for these either. It knows there are some journeys meant for you and others that aren't, and both outcomes are simply meant to be.

Growing into yourself is terrifying at times. All the pressure to find out who you are, what you like, our passions, your goals, your drive in life. It is overwhelming. No one teaches you to stop and breathe. No one teaches you that you will always be growing. The flowers grow, blossom, wilt, and return again. A constant life cycle of learning, of blooming, and so too do you.

You cannot physically see someone's heart from the outside. You don't know of the scars it bears or the stories it wants to share. But people often hint at the journey their hearts have taken. It's in their eyes when you offer kindness rather than anger. It's in the way they walk after you tell them to enjoy their day. It's in their smile when you offer a smile first. It's in their spirit when you acknowledge their worth.

I've been inhaling and exhaling and learning to let go of all the things that hold me back. I have been tending to my heart and listening to my soul, realizing to let go and to breathe is the first step in becoming whole.

We speak of mountains and the bravery of climbing them. Of the challenge we face with them, of the power they hold over our becoming. We forget the road we took to reach the mountain; we forget the courage it took to attempt the road to the mountain. We forget the sleepless night before, when we willed ourselves to take the road to the mountain to climb it. There are so many steps you take before attempting any hurdle, any challenge. You should be proud for even rising to climb the mountain.

The world moves so fast, sometimes it is impossible to breathe. When this happens, remind yourself to feel the air around you, the way it kisses your skin. Remind yourself to notice the ground beneath you, the grass, the pavement, the sound of your footsteps. Notice every color in the sky, the birds, the clouds, the sun and stars. Remind yourself of the gratitude you have for every single breath.

Life is meant to be more than dreams and aspirations and busy days. Life is meant to be noticed, to be absorbed, to be treasured. Notice when the sun catches the glass of your window, when the birds call out in the trees, when the waves crash into the shore, when the clouds part to reveal the moon. More than that, notice the person who lets you cut in line, the delivery driver who asks about your day, the friend who calls to see how you are, the wish you made late at night upon the brightest star. Life is meant to be noticed, not wasted away.

When you breathe, breathe deeply; and when you laugh, laugh from the depths of your soul. When you love, love with all your heart. When you are hurting, feel the pain, understand it, and let it go.

Things will feel different someday.
Your breath won't catch every time
you hear their name
and see an old photograph
or old message.
You will feel free, healed, moved on.

I have memorized your heartbeat in the way I have memorized the lyrics to my favorite song. I know the patterns of your breathing, the touch of your skin. I know your scent; it tastes like Sunday morning. I know my love for you is greater than all the stars burning.

The first moment I saw you, I forgot to breathe. The first moment you spoke, I forgot to breathe. The first moment you kissed me, held my hand, told me you loved me, I forgot to breathe. But the moment you told me I was everything you had been hoping to find was the first time I breathed instead of forgetting.

Make space for the ache
live with it
collect yourself slowly
face every moment with it
choose to breathe through it

And more than anything, I hope you will find someone who reminds you to breathe. Who understands all your dreams, your needs, and insecurities. Who doesn't try to push you to be someone you are not. Because you deserve that kind of support, that adoring love, that breath of fresh air.

If they say you are broken, just know your soul was never meant to be perfect; it was always meant to split and to splinter, so that the light could shine through.

Your hand is meant for my hand.
Your lips meant for my lips.
Your heart meant for my heart.
Your soul meant for my soul.

Your whole being
meant for taking
my breath away.

I have been at war with myself for such a long time, the moments of insecurity, of doubt, of wondering if anything about me is ever good enough. I have found myself at the place falling stars return dreams, where forests become homes for the lost and weary. I am always gently reminding myself each breath carries worth. Each heartbeat carries value. Each small triumph the greatest I will ever know.

Find the place that helps you recover and go there as surely as you need it. Use this place to breathe courage back into your soul, to lay all the burdens of the day to rest. To acknowledge any heartache or moments of yourself you believed less. No matter how difficult some hours, or days, or weeks feel, know that this is your safe space, your place to rest, recover, and heal.

It can take years for someone to know their worth. To validate themselves in the way they deserve. To acknowledge their strengths, accept their flaws, look forward to every new day. It can take scars and bruises and battles to finally realize we make ourselves whole. So, if you are lucky enough to have a hand reach for you, reach back in kindness. Don't undo all the work someone has put into their soul.

Here you are thinking about all the things that have broken you, left you hanging by threads. Forced you to crawl into a cave so deep with so many words left unsaid. But you forget about all the things you still have. You forget that the person steering the ship is you. You forget that these things broke you but they did not destroy you.

You are still here.

Inhale the morning light as fully as you can, embrace
the things to come, the dreams to be had, the goals to be
won. Welcome the love in your heart as much as you have
welcomed the sun.

We aren't made to always be full of energy; we can't always be the light or the storyteller or the life of the whole room and party. You are allowed days to feel exhausted, to feel as though your bones are too heavy and your voice cracks open with insecurities every time you speak. You don't have to always be the shoulder for someone else to lean on. You are still worthy even when you don't feel like smiling; you are still strong even when all you want to do is stay in bed. Sometimes the world expects too much. Sometimes we are all guilty of forgetting we are all just human.

I will be honest, I am still learning how to breathe steadily when my path leads me through things I cannot control. I am still learning to let go of the things that do not add to my own value. I am still learning to listen to my heart every time it says to slow down. I am still learning that while the leaves may fall, they will grow once more.

You have this heart, and it wants to be loved and to be told it is the first choice. To be respected, promised things that aren't broken, adored in the way it should be adored. And I know it hasn't been easy; there have been moments so unkind and unforgiving, so devastating. But this does not diminish your heart, the wonder that it holds, or the strength it has to endure such disappointments. You have a beautiful heart; I just wanted you to know.

It takes disaster, brokenness, chaos to realize the value in this world. If only people would look at the stars more, stare up into the deepest parts of the universe, and see just how vast, how fleeting, how all-encompassing life really is. Maybe we would all live a little differently.

The breathing will be shaky, uncontrollable, sharp. But then it will become steady, in control, free. It is important to breathe through the anxiety, breathe through the panic, keep breathing to reach the place of peace.

A whole world exists in every inhale and every exhale. It is filled with compassion and understanding. It is filled with hopes that you stay and that you continue forward. Which is why you must always continue breathing, always continue inhaling and exhaling.

If your soul needs a friend

Even when you have no reason, and the world no longer feels like the place you want to be, remember there is someone here hoping for you. Someone here in your corner, and that person is me.

It's three in the morning, and we are all together in this heartache.

You can weather every storm that comes your way. But just in case you need a little encouraging, remember there is a lighthouse atop every hill, wishing the best for your soul and its strength, its courage, its very will.

If you are wondering why the earth still hopes to see you smile or the flowers rise again to hear your dreams, know that it is because without you the universe stops spinning.

There are lyrics that will make you feel things and movies that will make your heart beat fast. There are bright colors lighting up the sky, laughter in the middle of crowded rooms, people to tell you that they miss you, moments when you will be reminded of the unconditional love you have. There are cities to be lost in, museums to take in, traveling to be ventured, roads to be taken, conversations to be had. There are so many things ahead of you. So many reasons to stay.

When thinking about the days ahead, just remember that worry will not bring closure, and guilt will not ease the past. You must move forward and follow your heart.

You are brave for rising out of bed when you don't feel you can. You are brave for choosing to live, even when you have no reason to. You are brave for sharing your story in the hopes it may help someone else. So, if no one has told you how brave you are today, I hope you know how brave I think you are.

Don't make your body the enemy. It is your map, your home, your canvas, your certainty. It deserves to be told it is beautiful, even on the days you notice every stretch mark and scar. Your body is the vessel for your soul; it is an entire earth of your being.

You have spent too long in the spaces between longing and dreaming. If you needed a sign to start accomplishing rather than fantasizing, this is it.

It doesn't matter to me what books you read or movies you love. It doesn't matter the clothes you wear; the color of your hair, eyes, or skin; when you end or where you begin. It doesn't matter where you come from, where you are headed, how many tears you have cried, the things you have laughed over, the places you have been. All that matters are the moments you stayed true to yourself, what you wanted, how you grew, how you replenished your soul.

If you have done something kind today, or beautiful, or accomplished a goal you never thought you would, I am proud of you. Even if you think no one notices or cares for all the wins you have, know that you are still doing bright things. Know that everything you do and all that you have achieved matters.

It takes many hands to build skyscrapers that stand tall against the skyline. Just like it takes many kind words to build someone up. Tell people they are magic; watch them stand tall against their own skylines.

The thoughts sometimes feel like too much rain, hurtling down so heavily, they're almost drowning you. But look up to the sky; tell the dark, angry clouds you are not afraid. Tell the whole damn universe you are the king or queen of your story and no one can strip you of your bravery.

I knew someone once who had become so damaged, she
no longer knew how to respond to kindness or the love she
deserved. But she's older now, a little wiser, a lot stronger.
And she knows the strength she has, the fire in her bones. She
is more than I ever imagined, more than I ever could have
hoped to have known.

We let ourselves go sometimes. The real defeat is when we punish ourselves for our setbacks rather than applauding ourselves for starting fresh again.

And in the moments you have no one to turn to, look out to the open sky and know there are billions of stars burning just to see you make it until the morning. The stars are rooting for you.

People tell you that you have to have everything figured out or your life won't have meaning. But it's not true. You can be lost and worthy at the same time.

We make so many promises to ourselves, it's impossible to keep all of them. It doesn't mean we have failed if we forget to take the trash out, or make the bed, or wash the dishes, finish the report, fill the car with gas, do the assignment, or return the voice mail. If we accomplished everything in one day, there would be no purpose for tomorrow, and there is always purpose for tomorrow.

Some moments have to happen so they may shape you, teach you, undo you, and remake you.

Being honest about how you feel is a very brave thing. And it's not like you can plan it for weeks and months and suddenly everything comes tumbling out in a perfectly rehearsed way. Because life doesn't work like that. You could be standing in front of your deepest fears and, after baring your soul, feel foolish and embarrassed. You'll go home to cry into your pillow or call your best friend, who will tell you not to worry and that nothing is your fault. But you are missing the point. It's not how perfectly you faced your fears, it's that you had the courage to face them in the first place. That's worth going home for. That's something to be proud of.

If you are struggling to be who you are, if you feel shame for loving who you love, if you believe there will never be a place in this world for you, know that you belong here, that your soul is loved. That on the days you feel most alone, you can always come to these pages and know that you are home.

I hope you never diminish your strength or worth just to fit into the rhythm of the world. I hope you embrace your wildest dreams and chase the love you know will make your hands shake and your knees weak. I hope you climb, soar, dive into all the goals you want to achieve. I hope you never lose sight of why you started or where you're headed. I hope you always grow, flourish, continue to become stronger. I hope you know I'll always be cheering you, I'll always be your friend, I'll always be in your corner.

I think of you in the way I think of the moon. I don't always see its beauty; I don't always catch its light through my window. But I *know* of its beauty, of its worth, and I am in awe of the way it shines. Every night, always and forever.

These are for your soul

I didn't think I would know the difference between holding a hand and holding a soul, until that day we drove a stretch of highway and you had one hand on the wheel and the other over mine; and somehow, I felt your love in my bones.

Young

We were teenagers,
> living each day in a dream, calling each other in the
> middle of the night
> under bedsheets and giggling when we first said,
>> "I love you"

A Little Older

We had our first fight,
> in the rain.
> I cried, and you were silent, not knowing what to do.
> Our paths started going separate ways, even though
> our love was still so true.

Older

We often think of those moments
> when we were young, carefree, drunk on love.
> But it's different now, stronger.
> Two paths went and came back together,
> as all souls do when they are meant to be.

We find life difficult at times, perplexing even. We try to avoid the things that make us sad, angry, frustrated. But we learn these things aren't easily avoided. Life is built up of moments, each fulfilling in their own way. The healing comes from being able to recognize it's okay to feel the emotions as they happen. If you are sad, feel sad. If you are confused, feel confused. If you are happy, feel happy. Because each moment passes, the good and the bad.

So, I hope that years from now, when you're sitting at the kitchen table and it's cold outside but you're wearing my sweater, I'll be standing in the doorway with cups of coffee and unedited manuscripts. You'll smile at me and ask me about my day, and I'll say I'm glad to be home with you. I hope all our healing leads me to a life we both love.

Maybe it's not about whether you fly or fall. It's how humble you are when you fly and how gracious you are when you fall.

There are some things I am afraid of, like closed spaces and lonely nights and strange, dark places. But if I am truly honest, what scares me the most is if you were to peel away all my layers and untangle all my secrets, you would find the deepest parts of me were not what you wanted. I am afraid that everything I hold inside is not what you are looking for.

Self-love means something different to everyone. How someone shows love to themselves may not be the same way you show love to yourself. But it's more about the conversation, the one you have in the quiet hours with your own thoughts. The way you start to show yourself a little more compassion. The way you gently remind yourself things will be okay on the days it feels everything is crashing and slipping away.

One of the greatest riddles in life is, as humans, we live through many things. Some things we wish we had never done, because they break us in ways we feel we'll never survive. Other things we wish we could repeat again and again, just to get the same feeling. Some we've forgotten, stored deep away in our minds. Others we play like a record, never wanting it to end. But granted, all these moments make us who we are. They remind us we are still here existing. They plant smiles across our faces, make us cry, leave fires burning in our hearts. They are the key to who we are. If you reversed these moments, you wouldn't be the person you are.

When someone betrays your trust, leaves you in pieces and broken on the floor, it becomes difficult to open yourself up to others again. But don't let this harden your heart. Not everyone is selfish or only thinks of themselves. There are people out there who will say, "I believe in my happiness, but I also believe in yours."

You will wake up in the middle of the night, drowning in thoughts of what could have been. But in the morning, it's important to rise again, dust off the heartache, and understand that, despite the setbacks, you will survive the pain.

It feels nice just to disconnect sometimes. The other day, I spent the late morning sitting on my parents' front steps. I watched the birds come and go from the tree in their front yard. It's full of flowers, the petals falling because summer is turning into fall. I watched the ants crawl along the pavement, over hurdles that, to tiny life, probably feel great, and I reminded myself it's okay not to know it all. The cars moved along the road, beyond the fence, holding people all with lives probably different than my own. But breathing in the air around me gave me purpose, strength in my heart, a home.

All the memories
    feel like broken glass on my skin
    but I am shedding every layer
    to start again

I have these scars
    from the marks you left
    all over my heart

You abandoned our love
    and discarded
    all our plans

People remind me to forget
    about you and all the hope
    I placed in your arms

But a war isn't won by forgetting
    Instead I'll hit back hard
    take back the air you stole
    from my lungs

And remind myself
    homes are rebuilt over ashes

It's not all about being patient with yourself, but also others. It's finding the courage to say what does and doesn't make you comfortable and allowing someone else to understand those boundaries. When a person has only known one way of thinking their whole life, you can't expect them to change overnight. Patience helps.

I met a girl once; she said her greatest dream was to be a dancer. I met a boy once; he said his greatest dream was to be an astronaut. Now I like to think, perhaps one day they will meet, and I'll see them on those starry nights, dancing on the moon.

Whether you blame yourself or somebody else, it won't help you. Blame is not a bandage; it doesn't heal wounds. Instead it makes the skin rot, waste away in anger. Letting go of the blame doesn't mean you are forgetting; it means you are moving on from the things you find upsetting.

Maybe letting go is really a muscle we need to build. The ghosts of our past weigh so heavy, they become difficult to carry. Instead of holding on, if we learn to let go more regularly, perhaps our souls will feel lighter, stronger, more in control.

It is difficult to choose ourselves, but not always selfish. Despite wanting to be good to everybody, sometimes you need to start being good to yourself. There is no shame in wanting to choose your happiness. There is no shame in wanting the flowers in your garden to grow again. You are allowed to move your own needs to the top of the priority list.

You should make time for the things you enjoy. Playing Scrabble, walking in the sunshine, reading books, and turning the music up loud. You don't have to always follow the crowd; sometimes enjoying the things you love most is the most beautiful thing about you.

It feels good when you accomplish things. It doesn't matter how simple or complex those things may be, it's the feeling you get afterward. You learn to ride a bike, you finish your essay, you graduate, or start your own business; it's all the same. Sometimes even just rising out of bed is enough accomplishment for one day.

Live with intention. When you have purpose to seek things greater and more meaningful in life, you find your heart beats a little faster.

All the museums in the world, and I wonder most about the one I would have for myself. Clustered in between my heart and soul. What I would fill it with, paintings of the moments I chose to be bold. Sculptures of the people I have loved. Artifacts of the history I have built from my life. And if anyone discovered this museum, would they visit again? More importantly, would I be on the front steps, welcoming them in?

Maybe our destiny has already been written, maybe it
hasn't. Maybe we run on two parallel lines, or maybe we are
constantly shifting, changing, just a giant scribble on a page.
But I like to think I have a choice of the person I will be. I
know I always have the choice to treat others compassionately.

The universe can be cruel, and it can be kind
But balance starts with yourself,
in the heart, in the mind, and in the soul

It's about understanding you are not a burden. You are made up of thoughts and feelings and skin that sometimes scars and bones that sometimes ache. You live through journeys by forgiving yourself for your mistakes. You become a better you when you accept rawness and honesty and reject any thoughts that you are a monstrosity.

You are so beautiful when you glow
the way your soul reaches your eyes
I hope that for all your life
you continue to shine

When I made it home again, from all the anger and the pain, I promised myself I would allow a special place in my heart reserved for me. In this space, I would fill it with gentle reminders that I am more than the doubt and negativity. I would hang pictures in the space of the dreams and goals I had, and I would always make sure the fire was burning, always forgiving, always learning.

More often than not, it is not advice we seek but rather just someone to listen us. The world is made up of people with opinions and stories to share, but what is the worth of those stories if we have no one to listen to them? And in the end, always know that you will have someone in the world listening to you, cherishing your stories, and hoping you make your way back home. Hoping you always remember, you are never alone.

It won't be easy, putting yourself back together again. You'll feel the hurt, like you feel whiskey as it burns your throat. You'll want to take back all the things you ever said and the love letters you wrote. You'll have sleepless nights, play sad songs on the radio, and try to forget all the memories folding into you. But you are much more than the heartache. You are stronger than the grief that consumes you. Often when sadness knocks at our door, it wants to be embraced rather than turned away. Hold your sadness; let it stay awhile. Whisper that things will work themselves out and, despite the clouds, you'll learn again to smile.

It's beautiful to have a heart that allows us to love, lungs that allow us to breathe air when it's about to rain, and a mind that allows us to think and feel so deeply for things. Sometimes we don't realize it's enough just to be human. It's enough just to have a soul.

When I first sat down to write the final chapter in the Pillow Thoughts series, it felt like I had come full circle. What started as a small book of feelings turned into a series full of not only hope for myself but also hope I now have for all of you. I wanted to thank you for all the support you have shown this series and for sharing your stories with me over the last four years. It has been an adventure I will never forget. I look forward to continuing on in the Pillow Thoughts universe and whatever adventures that may lead to. For now, no matter where the seas and skies take you, always know you have a friend in the jellyfish, the heart, the owl, and the fox. May you, your heart, mind, and soul always flourish; may you dream and heal and look forward to every morning. You will always have a home in my heart and a cup of tea waiting.

Yours forever and always,
        Courtney

Thank you for reading this book.
I hope you enjoyed reading it as much as I enjoyed writing it.

You can view more of my work on Twitter @CourtPeppernell
and Instagram @courtneypeppernell.

Feel free to write to me via courtney@pepperbooks.org.

Pillow Thoughts App now available on iOS and Android—
download yours today!

Pillow Thoughts IV

Andrews McMeel Publishing
a division of Andrews McMeel Universal
1130 Walnut Street, Kansas City, Missouri 64106

www.andrewsmcmeel.com

22 23 24 25 26 VEP 10 9 8 7 6 5 4 3

ISBN: 978-1-5248-5452-2

Library of Congress Control Number: 2020934877

Editor: Patty Rice
Art Director/Designer: Diane Marsh
Production Editor: Elizabeth A. Garcia
Production Manager: Cliff Koehler

Illustrations by Justin Estcourt

ATTENTION: SCHOOLS AND BUSINESSES
Andrews McMeel books are available at quantity discounts with bulk purchase for educational, business, or sales promotional use. For information, please e-mail the Andrews McMeel Publishing Special Sales Department: specialsales@amuniversal.com.